Happy Independence Day

First Edition

NEWMAN SPRINGS PUBLISHING
320 Broad Street
Red Bank, NJ 07701

First originally published by Newman Springs Publishing 2023

ISBN 979-8-88763-551-4 (Paperback)
ISBN 979-8-89308-047-6 (Hardcover)
ISBN 979-8-88763-553-8 (Digital)

Printed in the United States of America

Happy Independence Day

Melanie Romero

Acknowledgments

I would like to take a moment to dedicate my first illustration to all those who have fought and died for our country. Thank you for your service. You will never be forgotten. And to our President of the United States, Joe Biden, and former President Barack Obama, for bringing change and pride back to our country and keeping the spirit of America burning. Last but not least, I could never forget the main two apples of my eyes that have always shined and kept my head to the sky: Colonel Gertrude, United States Army; and Master Sergeant Miranda, United States Marines. THANK YOU! Stay *fine*!

Boys are playing in the backyard.

One little boy yells, “What’s the big deal about Independence Day?”

Another little boy responds, “You mean you don’t know!? Well, let me tell you.”

As the little boy walks up, the rest of the boys begin to huddle around so they can hear the story.

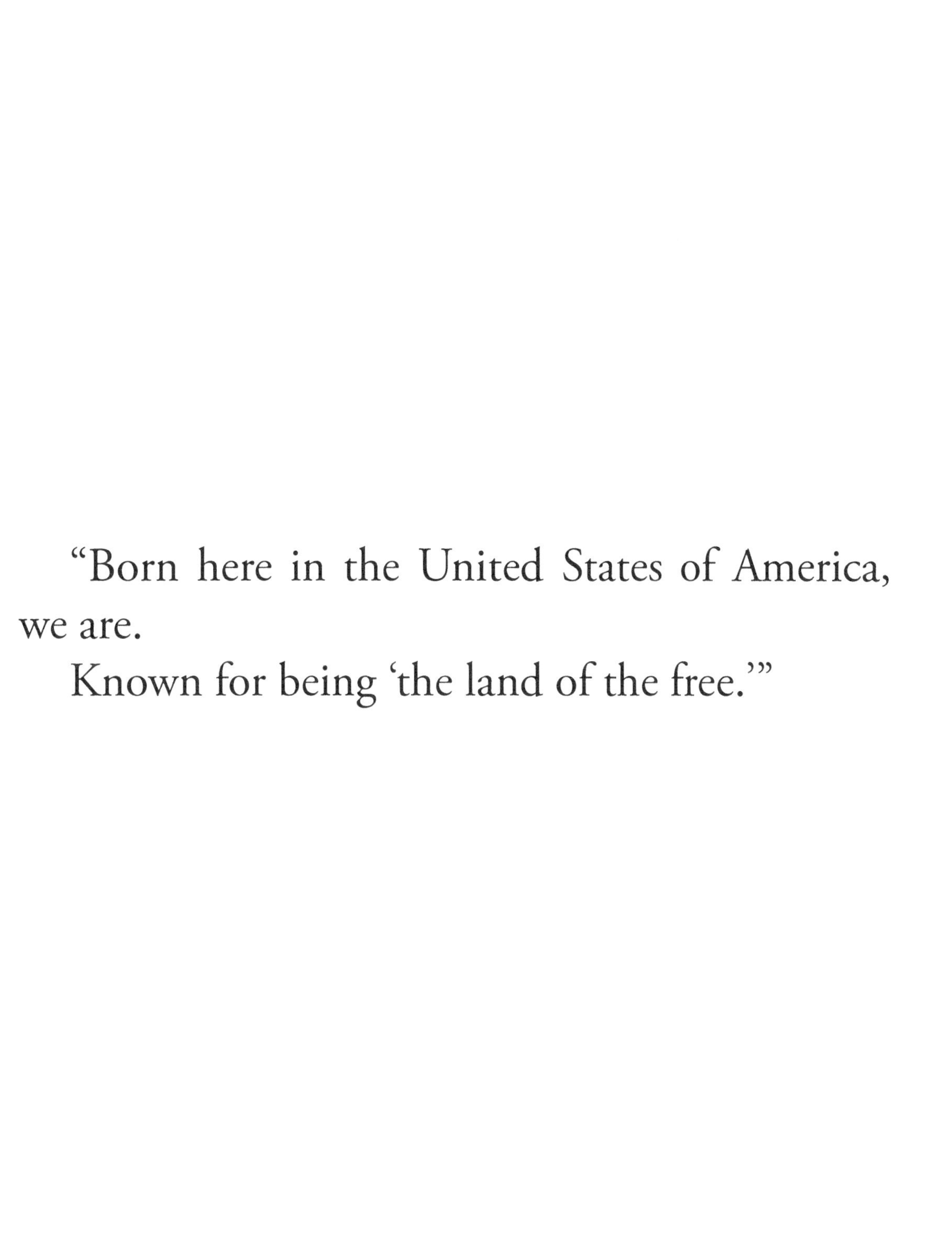

"Born here in the United States of America, we are.

Known for being 'the land of the free.'"

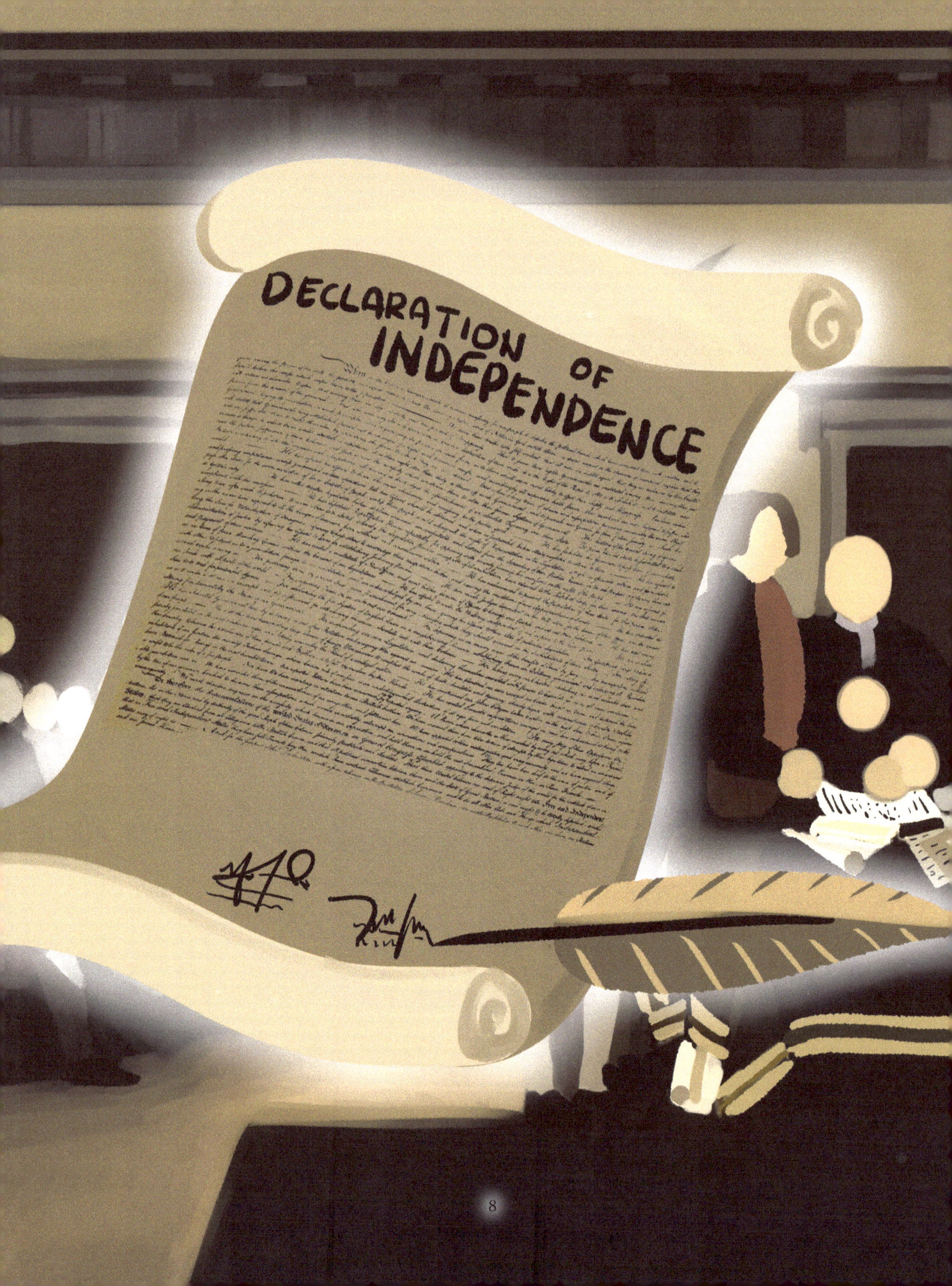

DECLARATION OF INDEPENDENCE

“But why?” the little boy asks.

“Let me explain. On July 4, 1776, the Declaration of Independence announced our liberty, which is our freedom. All men are created equally, and the separation from Great Britain.

So we celebrate our *independence*. Happy Independence Day!"